Summer Olympic Games

Athens, Greece: 1896, 2004
Paris, France: 1900, 1924
St Louis, USA: 1904
London, England: 1908, 1948
Stockholm, Sweden: 1912
Antwerp, Belgium: 1920
Amsterdam, Holland: 1928
Los Angeles, USA: 1932, 1984
Berlin, Germany: 1936
Helsinki, Finland: 1952
Melbourne, Australia: 1956
Rome, Italy: 1960
Tokyo, Japan: 1964
Mexico City, Mexico: 1968
Munich, Germany: 1972
Montreal, Canada: 1976
Moscow, USSR: 1980
Seoul, Korea: 1988
Barcelona, Spain: 1992
Atlanta, USA: 1996
Sydney, Australia: 2000
Beijing, China: 2008

Winter Olympic Games

Chamonix, France: 1924
St Moritz, Switzerland: 1928, 1948
Lake Placid, USA: 1932, 1980
Garmisch-Partenkirchen, Germany: 1936
Oslo, Norway: 1952
Cortina d'Ampezzo, Italy: 1956
Squaw Valley, USA: 1960
Innsbruck, Austria: 1964, 1976
Grenoble, France: 1968
Sapporo, Japan: 1972
Sarajevo, Yugoslavia: 1984
Calgary, Canada: 1988
Albertville, France: 1992
Lillehammer, Norway: 1994
Nagano, Japan: 1998
Salt Lake City, USA: 2002
Turin, Italy: 2006
Vancouver, Canada: 2010

P9-CNI-954

796.4809 GUI
History of the Olympic Games
Guile, Melanie
Copy No: 1 BookID: 170675.01
340340348666

History of the Olympic Games

Melanie Guile

MELVILLE SENIOR HIGH SCHOOL LIBRARY
170675

Heinemann
LIBRARY

First published in 2008 by Heinemann Library,
an imprint of Pearson Australia Group Pty Ltd,
20 Thackray Road, Port Melbourne
Victoria 3207 Australia

Visit the Heinemann Library website
www.heinemannlibrary.com.au

© Pearson Education Australia 2008
(a division of Pearson Australia Group Pty Ltd,
ABN 40 004 245 943)

12 11 10 09 08
10 9 8 7 6 5 4 3 2 1

Reproduction and Communication for educational purposes

The Australian *Copyright Act 1968* (the Act)
allows a maximum of one chapter or 10 per cent
of the pages of this work, whichever is the greater,
to be reproduced and/or communicated by any
educational institution for its educational purposes
provided that the educational institution (or the body
that administers it) has given a remuneration notice
to Copyright Agency Limited (CAL) under the Act.

For details of the CAL licence for educational
institutions contact:
Copyright Agency Limited
Level 15, 233 Castlereagh Street
Sydney NSW 2000
Telephone: (02) 9394 7600
Facsimile: (02) 9394 7601
Email: info@copyright.com.au

Reproduction and Communication for other purposes

Except as permitted under the Act (for example,
a fair dealing for the purposes of study, research,
criticism or review) no part of this book may
be reproduced, stored in a retrieval system,
communicated or transmitted in any form or by
any means without prior written permission. All
enquiries should be made to the publisher at the
address above.

Commissioning: Michelle Freeman and Sarah Russell
Editorial: Eliza Collins
Cover and text design: Anne Donald
Map and diagram illustration: Anne Donald
Picture/permissions research: Jes Senbergs and
Wendy Duncan
Production: Tracey Jarrett

Typeset in Syntax 12/17 pt
Pre-press by Publishing Pre-press, Port Melbourne
Printed in Singapore by Craft Print International
Limited
The paper used to print this book comes from
sustainable resources.

**National Library of Australia
Cataloguing-in-Publication data:**

Guile, Melanie, 1949– .
Olympic Games 2008: history of the Olympic
Games.

Bibliography.
Includes index.
For primary school students.
ISBN 9781740703734 (hbk).

1. Olympic Games (29th : 2008 : Beijing, China)
– Juvenile literature. 2. Olympics – History -
Juvenile literature. I. Title.

796.48

Acknowledgements

The publisher would like to thank the following for
permission to reproduce copyright material: Ancient
Art & Architecture Collection Ltd: p. **12**, /Ronald
Sheridan: p. **15**; Corbis/Bettmann: pp. **5**, **14**, **16**,
25, /Gianni Dagli Orti: pp. **9**, **13**, /Wally McNamee:
p. **23**; Getty Images: p. **18**, /Hulton Archive: p. **17**,
/Kazuhiro Nogi: p. **19**; photolibrary/Alamy/Ace
Stock Limited: pp. **10**, **11**, /George Blonsky: p. **27**,
/Superstock, Inc: p. **24**. All other images PhotoDisc.

Cover photograph of a figure from an ancient Greek
vase reproduced with permission of photolibrary/
Alamy/Ace Stock Limited.

Every attempt has been made to trace and
acknowledge copyright. Where an attempt has been
unsuccessful, the publisher would be pleased to hear
from the copyright owner so any omission or error
can be rectified.

Disclaimer

All the Internet addresses (URLs) given in this book
were valid at the time of going to press. However,
due to the dynamic nature of the Internet, some
addresses may have changed or ceased to exist
since publication. While the author and publisher
regret any inconvenience this may cause readers, no
responsibility for any such changes can be accepted
by either the author or the publisher.

Contents

Words that are printed in bold, **like this**,
are explained in the Glossary on page 31.

Ancient Greece and the Olympic Games

The Olympic Games are one of the most important sporting competitions in the world today. Since 1896, the modern Olympic Games, as we know them, have been held every four years – except during the two world wars in 1916, 1940 and 1944. However, the Olympic Games are much older.

The first Olympic Games

The Olympic Games started before 1300 BCE – more than 3300 years ago – in a place called Olympia in Greece. Historians think that the first games began as **religious festivals**, or celebrations, for the king of the Greek gods, Zeus. The Greeks believed Zeus fought a great fight at Olympia and won power over the world there. Olympia became a special place where people prayed to Zeus and held sports competitions in his **honour**. Popular sports at Olympia were running, wrestling and racing with horses and **chariots**, or two-wheeled carts. Sports champions were great heroes. The original Olympic Games were held regularly for around 500 years and then died out – no one knows why.

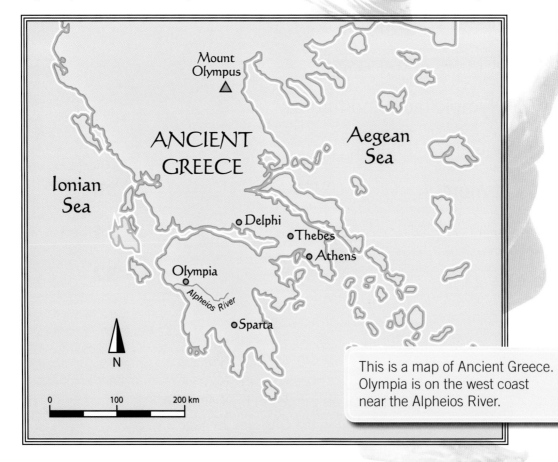

Mount Olympus △

ANCIENT GREECE

Aegean Sea

Ionian Sea

o Delphi

o Thebes

o Athens

Olympia o

Alpheios River

o Sparta

N

0   100   200 km

This is a map of Ancient Greece. Olympia is on the west coast near the Alpheios River.

A new start

About 3000 years ago, in 800 BCE, King Iphitos of Elis decided to revive the Olympic Games. He invited sportsmen from cities all over Greece to come in peace to compete. The games were a success. By 776 BCE, the Olympics were the most important games in the world. Today, the games that King Iphitos restarted are known as the ancient Olympic Games.

The ancient Olympic Games

The **ancient** Olympic Games were held every four years in August and lasted for up to five days. Only men were allowed to compete or to watch. Events included foot races, long jumping, wrestling and boxing matches, and throwing a spear called a **javelin** and a round, flat piece of stone or metal called a **discus**. One event, the **pentathlon**, was made up of five sports – running, jumping, discus, javelin throwing and wrestling. Horse and chariot races were also held. The ancient Olympic Games became famous and lasted for nearly 1200 years.

A religious festival

To the ancient Greeks, sport was not only played for fun, but it was also part of their religion. Religious buildings, called **temples**, lay in the middle of the sports grounds of Olympia. Special **prayers**, or requests, and gifts, such as meat and wine, were offered to the gods before the games, and athletes had to promise to compete fairly to honour the gods. Winners said prayers of thanks.

Zeus was the king of the gods. The ancient Greeks believed that Zeus once wrestled his father, Kronos, for power over the world on a hill near Olympia.

Olympic fact

The Greeks had many gods, both male and female. They believed these gods looked and acted like human beings, but were stronger and more powerful. The Greeks felt that men could be like gods if they trained hard. Also, sportsmen believed that when they competed, they were pleasing the gods. So, for the ancient Greeks, sport and religion went together.

Olympia

Olympia is a village near the west coast of Greece. Today, Olympia is a collection of ruins, but in **ancient** times, it was a huge sports complex that was used every four years for the Olympic Games. Sportsmen came from all over Greece and nearby countries to compete at Olympia. It had training grounds, two racetracks, a swimming pool, and an area set aside for praying to the gods.

The **Temple** of Hera had 40 carved **columns**, or cylinders, made of stone.

The gymnasium was a large, open-air training ground where athletes practised running, **discus** and **javelin** throwing. It was surrounded by a covered area for **spectators**, or people who watched the events.

The *palaestra* was the training ground for wrestling and boxing.

Athletes bathed in the swimming pool. There were no swimming races at the ancient Olympic Games.

The *altis* was a special large area where the temples were located. Each side was 180 metres long. Before the games, the sportsmen gave gifts and offerings to the gods on an **altar**, or flat-topped stone, in the *altis*.

Stone starting lines marked each end of the track in the stadium. Grooves carved in the starting lines allowed runners to dig in their bare toes so they would not slip at the start of a race.

The stadium held competitions for discus and javelin throwing, wrestling, boxing, jumping and running. The straight track was 210 metres long and 32 metres wide. People watched from grassy slopes around the track.

The *zanes* were 16 metal statues of the god, Zeus, which lined the path the athletes used to enter the stadium. The statues reminded the sportsmen that they were competing for the gods.

The hippodrome was a large oval-shaped track for racing horses and two-wheeled carts called **chariots**.

The *bouleuterion* was a building where the sportsmen swore the Olympic **oath**, promising to obey the rules of the games.

The Temple of Zeus had tall stone columns holding up the roof and many carvings around the top. A huge statue of Zeus sitting on his throne was inside. The statue was 13 metres high and made of gold and **ivory**, which is made from the tusks of elephants.

Training for the ancient Olympic Games

To the **ancient** Greeks, sport was part of everyday life. Young men needed to be strong not only so they could fight in wars, but also to please the gods. Most cities in Greece had special training grounds where men exercised and practised different sports. Competitions were held on special occasions, such as funerals and religious holidays.

Many games

There were many different games held all over Greece. Famous games were held at places such as Delphi, Corinth and Nemea. There were even games especially for women. But the best athletes were sent to Olympia to compete in the Olympic Games.

Preparing for the Olympic Games

The ancient Greeks understood about training and health. They knew how important it was for sportsmen to eat lots of meat and cheese for building muscles. They also knew how to keep their skin healthy by bathing and rubbing their bodies with oil and sand to avoid sunburn.

Sportsmen practised hard under the strict eyes of their trainers, who were usually former champions. Olympic sportsmen trained for ten months in their home cities. Then, one month before the games, the trainers and sportsmen travelled to Olympia.

Olympic fact

Training in the sun was hot work. Outside the *palaestra* at Olympia was a swimming pool where the sportsmen cooled off. Before the sportsmen went into the water, they scraped the sand off their bodies with a metal tool called a **strigil**.

8

Facilities at Olympia

Olympia had special buildings and tracks where the athletes trained. The gymnasium was a large rectangular practice ground surrounded by covered areas. There was a running track along one side of the gymnasium and a large space in the middle for jumping and throwing **discus** and **javelin**. In bad weather, athletes and their trainers practised in the covered corridors around the edge of the running track.

Near the gymnasium was a smaller building called the *palaestra*, which was used for wrestling and boxing practice. It was designed like the gymnasium with an open ground surrounded by covered areas, although the ground was gravel, not grass. Before using the *palaestra*, wrestlers used a tool called a **pick** to crush any stones and make a smooth surface to practise on.

Judges

A group of ten men called *Hellanodikai* from Elis, a town near Olympia, watched the training. They checked that the athletes were good enough to compete and made sure they trained properly. The *Hellanodikai* also acted as judges during the games and had to swear an **oath**, promising to judge all athletes fairly.

Judges and trainers carried long sticks to hit any sportsman who broke the rules during a wrestling or boxing contest, known as a **bout**.

Competing at the ancient Olympic Games

The sporting competitions at the **ancient** Olympic Games were held over five days. Different kinds of events were held on each day, and every evening ended in celebrations. Time was also set aside for religious rituals. On the final day, when competition had finished, the winners were congratulated in a grand closing ceremony.

The opening ceremony

Religious ceremonies were an important part of the ancient Olympic Games. On the first day, sportsmen and their trainers went to a building called the *bouleuterion*. There, they swore an **oath** in front of a statue of Zeus, promising to obey the rules of the games. Then, each sportsman went to the *altis* and prayed to a favourite god to help him win.

Parade of champions

A man named Pelops was the first Olympic hero. He lived before 1500 BCE, and was famous for winning a great **chariot** race. When Pelops died, he was buried at Olympia.

Boys' competitions

The first day of competition was set aside for boys aged 12 to 18. There were boys' running races, and wrestling and boxing matches. Many of these junior champions went on to become Olympic champions in later years.

Horse races

Day two began with a parade of riders, horses and chariots into the horse-racing track called the hippodrome. Each lap of the track was about 1200 metres and races were up to 13 kilometres long. Events were fast and exciting – especially the chariot races. Chariots were small two-wheeled carts with two or four horses pulling them. Crashes were common, and many racers did not finish. Winners paraded at the end of the day, and prayers were sung to the chariot-racing hero, Pelops, whose statue stood in the grounds of Olympia.

Javelins are still thrown in the same way today as they were at Olympia.

Pentathlon

In the **pentathlon,** athletes competed in five different sports – long jumping, running, wrestling, and **discus** and javelin throwing. The discus was a round, flat piece of metal or stone, and the javelin was a kind of spear. The aim was to throw each of these objects a greater distance than anyone else.

Experts believe the long jump was like the modern triple jump. Athletes held weights in their hands to help them jump further. Next, was a short, fast running race called a **sprint**. If there was still no clear winner at the end of these events, a wrestling match was held to decide the winner.

Olympic fact

At the ancient Olympic Games, only the winners got a prize – a crown of olive leaves – but champions became rich in their home cities. For example, in 600 BCE, each Olympic champion was given 500 **drachmas** when he returned to his home town of Athens.

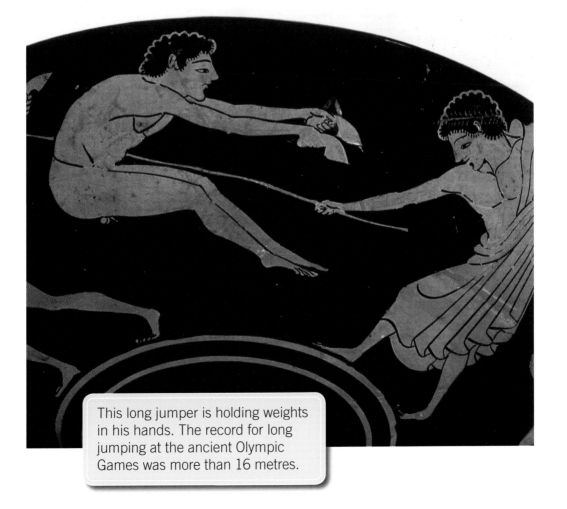

This long jumper is holding weights in his hands. The record for long jumping at the ancient Olympic Games was more than 16 metres.

Competing at the ancient Olympic Games

Parade

Day three began with a great parade of sportsmen and officials carrying gold and silver cups around the *altis*. Then, 100 bulls were led in and killed on an **altar**, or flat-topped stone, as a gift to the god, Zeus. Priests said **prayers** and offered meat and wine to the gods. After this religious ceremony, the foot races began.

The foot races

Running events were held in the stadium. Athletes lined up on the stone starting line, and races began at the blast of a trumpet. The long-distance race, the *dolikhos*, was around 4 kilometres, or about 20 laps. Twenty runners competed, and more than 20 000 people watched. There was also a race in **armour** where runners carried metal shields and wore helmets.

But the most important foot race was the **sprint**. This was called the *stade* and was run over about 200 metres, or one length of the stadium. The winner of the *stade* was the champion of the games. Like all the winners, he was given a purple ribbon as a prize, which he tied around his head or arms.

Parade of champions

Diagoras of Rhodes lived around 400 **BCE** and was a brilliant boxing champion at Olympia as well as many other **ancient** games. His sons and grandsons also became Olympic champions.

These men are running in the *hoplitodromos* race. They had to run two lengths of the stadium in armour.

Combat sports

Day four was set aside for the exciting **combat**, or fighting, sports – wrestling, boxing and the *pankration*. Wrestling events were very like they are today with different holds and throws. If a man's back or shoulders touched the ground three times, he lost the match. Boxing was the most dangerous sport. Fighters wore leather straps wrapped around their hands and threw punches mainly at the head. Boxing events were tough, and blood noses and other injuries were common. Matches lasted until one fighter gave in or got **knocked out**.

The *pankration* was a mix of boxing, wrestling and a street fight. Athletes could hit, kick and choke their **opponents**, or even break their fingers or toes. The **bout**, or contest, finished when one fighter admitted defeat.

Olympic fact

Pankration bouts were tough, but there were strict rules. For instance, it was within the rules to injure an opponent, but if he was killed, the dead man could be named the winner.

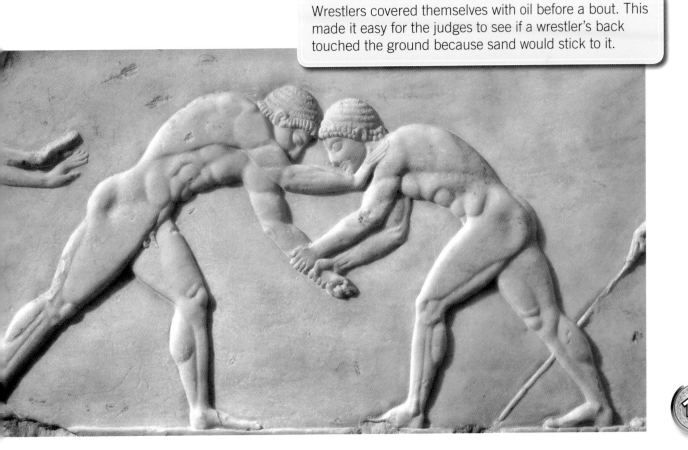

Wrestlers covered themselves with oil before a bout. This made it easy for the judges to see if a wrestler's back touched the ground because sand would stick to it.

13

The closing ceremony

Just as they do at the Olympic Games today, the **ancient** Olympic Games ended with a closing ceremony. It included presentations to the winners and a grand celebration.

Parade of winners

On day five of the games, all the winners walked in a grand parade to the **Temple** of Zeus in the *altis*. The *Hellanodikai* presented each winner with a crown made of olive leaves. There were no cash prizes or medals – the **honour** of winning was enough.

Closing feast

After the presentations, there was a huge feast. Everyone drank wine, ate food, sang songs and listened to poems, called **odes**, about other Olympic heroes. Sometimes, the celebrations lasted all night.

Parade of champions

Leonidas of Rhodes was the fastest man in the ancient world. He won all three running events at four Olympic Games from 164 to 152 BCE.

Olympic fact

This is part of an ode written by the famous poet, Pindar, in 476 BCE for Theron of Acragas who won the **chariot** race.

... what god, what hero, what man shall we celebrate? ... Theron must be **proclaimed** *[announced] because of his victorious four-horse chariot ... ocean breezes blow around the island of the blessed, and flowers of gold are blazing ... With these wreaths and garlands of flowers they* **entwine** *[wind around] their hands ...*

The leaves for the crown worn by this champion were cut from Zeus's special olive tree with a golden knife.

The end of the ancient Olympic Games

The Olympic Games became the most famous sporting contest in the ancient world, and many stories were written about them. The ancient Olympic Games were held from around 800 BCE to 388 AD and lasted nearly 1200 years, but then they came to an end.

Why the ancient Olympic Games ended

In 146 BCE, the **Romans** seized control of Greece by force when they **invaded** the country. The Romans enjoyed the Olympic Games, too, but they did not always follow the rules. Events became rougher, and cheating was common. Respect for the Olympic Games fell away, although they were still popular. Then, in the late 300s AD, the Romans changed to the **Christian** religion. The Olympic Games were a religious festival for the god Zeus, and Christians did not believe in him. So, in 393 AD, the Roman **emperor**, Theodosius I, banned the games. The Olympic Games were not held again for 1500 years.

Olympic fact

In 67 AD, the Roman emperor, Nero, decided to compete in the ancient Olympic Games. He gave the judges money so they would let him win the chariot race. Although Nero did not finish the race, the judges named him the winner!

Parade of champions

Milo of Kroton was a famous wrestling champion of the ancient Olympic Games. He ate 9 kilograms of meat, 9 kilograms of bread and 10 litres of wine every day to keep up his strength.

The ancient Greek goddess of victory was named Nike. The modern sports shoe company is named after her.

An historic discovery

For more than 1000 years, the Olympic Games were forgotten. Everyone thought the **ancient** stories and poems about them were just make believe. Then, in 1829, French **archaeologists** found the site of ancient Olympia. In 1875, a German team of **experts** dug up the site and discovered the remains of **temples**, gymnasiums, training grounds and racetracks. Interest in the ancient Olympic Games grew. In France, one man decided he would make the games live again.

Baron Pierre de Coubertin

Baron Pierre de Coubertin was a rich man who lived in Paris in the late 1800s. He loved sport. Baron de Coubertin believed that not only did sport make men and boys strong and healthy, but also that sporting competitions between countries helped to keep the peace between them.

In those days, sport was not played much in Europe. Baron de Coubertin wanted all countries to teach sport in schools as they did in England. He travelled around Europe and the USA, arranging competitions between countries. In 1892, Baron de Coubertin called a meeting of important people in Paris at which he explained his dream: 'the splendid … task of reviving the Olympic Games'.

Little interest

At first, no one was interested, but Baron de Coubertin did not give up. By 1894, at a meeting in Paris, five men – including the baron – formed a group called the International Olympic Committee (IOC). These men agreed to hold the first modern Olympic Games in 1896. Since the ancient Olympic Games were held in Greece, it seemed right to restart them in Athens.

Baron Pierre de Coubertin, the 'father of the modern Olympics', was born in Paris in 1863 and died in 1937.

16

The Athens Olympic Games

After many set-backs, including lack of money and arguments between officials, the first modern Olympic Games were held in Athens in April 1896. Modern events, such as cycling and swimming races, were held as well as ancient events, such as running and wrestling. Huge crowds came to watch, and the games were a great success.

The modern Olympic Games

Since 1896, the Olympic Games have been held every four years except during the two world wars (1914–1918 and 1939–1945). Some of the early games had confusing rules and dishonest judges, but the idea took hold. Today, the Olympic Games are famous around the world. They stand for peace and goodwill between countries as Baron de Coubertin hoped they would.

Parade of champions

American Robert Garrett had never thrown a real **discus** before competing in the 1896 Olympic Games. Garrett's style was clumsy, but he beat the experienced Greek discus throwers by 18 centimetres and won.

The first modern Olympic Games were watched by the king and queen of Greece. Americans won most of the events.

Olympic ideals

The **ancient** Olympic Games were much more than a sporting competition. Sportsmen had to come in peace, practise hard, play by the rules and offer **prayers** and gifts to the god-king Zeus. When Baron de Coubertin revived the games in the 1890s, he was inspired by these ancient Greek ideals. He wrote down a set of **noble**, or good and moral, rules that all Olympic athletes and trainers had to follow. Today, everyone who takes part in the Olympic Games is expected to live up to these ideals.

The five basic rules

In 1894, Baron de Coubertin wrote down five basic rules for the modern Olympic Games.

- The Olympic Games should be held every four years.

- Events should include modern sports.

- Only adults should compete.

- There should be no money given as prizes. Instead, the first three place-getters receive medals – gold for first, silver for second and bronze for third.

- Each Olympic Games should be held in a different country.

This photograph shows, from left, the silver, gold and bronze medals for the 2008 Beijing Olympic Games.

These athletes are being presented with their medals. Each gold medal must have at least 6 grams of real gold in it.

No pay

Initially, the International Olympic Committee (IOC) decided that all Olympic athletes should be **amateurs**. This means that the athletes play for the love of their sport, not money. This rule has caused many problems because many sportspeople are paid today – either by the businesses who support them or their governments who give them money to train. Now, the IOC has dropped the amateur rule to include these athletes. But, in the past, Olympic champions were banned from the Olympic Games for taking money, even at events held somewhere else.

Religion, peace, beauty

Baron de Coubertin wanted the Olympic Games to encourage three things – religion, peace and beauty. Like a religion, the Olympic Games have high ideals. The games aim to encourage peace by inviting all countries, even enemies, to come together to compete. They show the beauty of the human body in the brilliant skills of the athletes.

The Olympic motto

The Olympic **motto** is *Citius, Altius, Fortius*, which means 'Faster, Higher, Stronger' in **Latin**. It was chosen by Baron de Coubertin in 1894 at an 'international **congress**', or meeting, which he called in Paris to discuss restarting the Olympic Games.

Modern Olympic sports

Baron de Coubertin only included summer sports in the modern Olympic Games. However, the International Olympic Committee (IOC) soon noticed the increasing popularity of snow and ice sports. So, in 1924, the first winter Olympic Games were held at Chamonix in France. Today, there are 35 different sports in the summer and winter Olympic Games. Each group of sports has many different events. For example, the track-and-field group includes running, jumping and throwing events. Each host nation is allowed to choose one new sport to include in its Olympic Games. For instance, BMX bike events will feature for the first time at the Beijing Olympic Games in 2008.

Summer Olympic sports

At the summer Olympic Games, athletes compete in a wide range of competitions – on the track, in and on the water, in the open air and indoors. Only four sports have featured at every Olympic Games since 1896 – swimming, fencing, athletics and gymnastics. Some of the summer Olympic sports are described in detail on the following pages. The complete list of Summer Olympic sports is on the opposite page.

Aquatics

Aquatics are the water sports – diving, swimming, water polo and **synchronised** swimming. Water polo is a team sport where players try to throw a ball into a net at each end of the pool. Synchronised swimming, which used to be called 'water ballet', involves women performing moves music in pairs or teams to music.

Archery

Archers shoot at targets with bows and arrows, which can travel more than 240 kilometres per hour. The archer whose arrow lands closest to the centre of the target wins.

Badminton

Players hit a feathered ball called a **shuttlecock** backwards and forwards across a net using small racquets. Each run of successful hits is scored, and the highest score at the end of the match wins. Badminton is a fast and furious sport – players can cover more than 6 kilometres in a match.

Canoe and kayak

These boat races include events on smooth and rough water. This event was introduced to the summer Olympic Games in 1924. Women compete in the kayak events only.

Equestrian

These horse events include jumping in a show ring, cross-country racing – which is a three-day event – and **dressage**. 'Dressage' is a French word meaning 'training'. It is a kind of horse-and-rider ballet with graceful steps and moves to music.

Fencing

This sport is like sword fighting, but the swords are blunt. The winner is decided on the number of times each fencer touches the other with the weapon. Fencing is one of only four sports to feature at every modern Olympic Games.

Gymnastics

There are three different types of gymnastic events – trampoline, artistic gymnastics and rhythmic gymnastics. Artistic gymnasts use equipment such as rings, floor, beam, **vaulting** (jumping) boxes and bars. Rhythmic gymnasts use balls, ribbons, rope, clubs and hoops as they perform to music.

Handball

Handball began in Germany and was first played as an Olympic sport at the Berlin Olympic Games in 1936. Teams of seven players throw and pass a small ball on a court, trying to score goals by putting the ball between two posts.

Summer Olympic sports

aquatics

archery

athletics

badminton

baseball

basketball

boxing

canoe and kayak

cycling

equestrian

fencing

football (soccer)

gymnastics

handball

hockey

judo

modern **pentathlon**

rowing

sailing

shooting

softball

table tennis

taekwondo

tennis

triathlon

volleyball

weightlifting

wrestling

Modern Olympic sports

Judo

Judo is a hand-to-hand **combat** sport using hands and feet. It grew out of the Japanese combat sport, *jujitsu*, and relies on skill and balance rather than strength. Throwing an **opponent** to the floor usually wins most matches.

Modern pentathlon

For the modern **pentathlon**, athletes must compete in five different events – shooting, fencing, swimming, show jumping and running. This event was invented by Baron de Coubertin.

Rowing

Teams and individuals race in rowing boats. Events cover a range of distances and include different sizes of boats. Steve Redgrave of Great Britain is considered the world's greatest rower. He has won gold medals at the last five Olympic Games.

Softball

Softball has similar rules and format to baseball, except it is played with a larger ball. Olympic softball is played only by women. One softball **pitch**, or throw, was recorded at 118 kilometres per hour.

Triathlon

'Triathlon' is a Greek word meaning 'three contests'. Competitors have to race in three sports – swimming, cycling and running. Triathlon is a young sport – it started in the USA in 1974 and became an Olympic sport in 2000.

Volleyball

This is a team game where players punch a large ball backwards and forwards over a high net. Each rally is scored and the higher score wins. Beach volleyball is almost exactly the same, but it is played on sand. Beach volleyball first appeared as an Olympic event in Atlanta in 1996 and quickly became very popular with **spectators**.

Winter Olympic sports

The winter Olympic Games feature seven different sports. All events are played on ice or snow, both indoors and outdoors.

Biathlon

The word 'biathlon' means 'two contests'. Each athlete competes in cross-country skiing and rifle shooting.

Bobsleigh

This sport is like **toboggan** racing in which a long, narrow sled is used. Bobsleigh competitors sit in large sleds that slide down a steep, winding ice track.

Curling

Curling is an indoor sport. Two four-person teams use a long-handled pusher to slide stones across the ice so that they land in rings marked on the ice. The winning team has the stone nearest to the centre of the circle. Curling began in Scotland almost 500 years ago.

Ice hockey

This is hockey played on ice. Players wear skates and use hockey sticks and a flat sliding disc called a puck instead of a ball. Two 12-person teams try to get the puck into goals at each end. There are men's and women's teams.

Luge

Luge is like bobsleighing except each sled carries a single person who lies face up. Luge sleds are small and very fast.

Skating

Ice skating sports include speed skating races on a circular track and graceful figure skating and ice dancing.

Skiing

Skiing events include cross-country and downhill skiing, ski jumping and snowboarding. Ski jumping involves jumping off large ramps high into the air. Snowboarding is like skateboarding on snowy slopes and the competitors do flips in the air.

Luge has been an Olympic sport since 1964. Luge is the French word for 'sled'.

Disputes and disasters

Since the first modern Olympic Games were held in Athens in 1896, many things have gone wrong. Sometimes, there were problems with athletes or judges cheating. But, there have also been more serious problems, such as **terrorism** and **racism**. However, in spite of these events, the Olympic Games have grown stronger over the years.

Unfair

During the 1908 London Olympic Games, the English judges were not always fair because they were jealous of the Americans' success in track-and-field events. In the 400 metres race, the judges said the winner, American J. C. Carpenter, had run out of his lane even though no lanes were marked. The judges banned Carpenter from a re-run, and the other American athletes walked out in protest.

Hitler's games

The Berlin Olympic Games of 1936 were held in Germany, which was ruled by Adolf Hitler. Hitler and his **Nazi** followers were racists who believed white people were better than any other race. But, the best runner at those games was a brilliant African-American athlete named Jesse Owens. Hitler was not happy and refused to greet any black athlete who won an event

American Jesse Owens won the 100 metres, 200 metres, 400 metres relay and the long jump at the Berlin Olympic Games in 1936.

Masked terrorists kidnapped members of the Israeli wrestling and weightlifting teams in 1972. Since this event, Olympic Villages have been made much safer.

Terrorist attack

On 5 September 1972, eight **Palestinians** attacked the Israeli team in the Olympic Village at Munich in West Germany. The terrorists killed two Israelis straightaway and held another nine athletes **hostage**. All the remaining Israelis were murdered by the terrorists when a rescue bid by West German police failed. Five of the attackers and one policeman were also killed. This has been the worst **tragedy** of the modern Olympic Games.

Politics and sport

The Olympic Games are meant to encourage peace between countries, but that has not always been the case. In 1980, the USA withdrew from the Moscow Olympic Games to protest at the Soviet Union's (now Russia) **invasion** of Afghanistan. Sixty other countries, including Canada and China, joined the ban. In response, the Soviet Union and 13 other **communist** countries – including East Germany and Poland – **boycotted**, or refused to attend, the 1984 Los Angeles Games held by the Americans.

Atlanta bombing

On the night of 27 July 1996, during the Atlanta Olympic Games in the USA, a bomb exploded in Centennial Olympic Park among a crowd at a rock concert. Two people died and 111 were injured. The bomber was Eric Rudolph, an American terrorist. Rudolph was not caught until 2003, after he had exploded three more bombs across the USA.

Olympic facts and figures

The **motto** of 'Faster, Higher, Stronger' certainly rings true when you look at the amazing achievements of many of the athletes who have performed on the Olympic stage. Here are just some of the remarkable facts and figures from the modern Olympic Games.

The largest number

In 2004, 202 countries and 10500 athletes competed at the summer Olympic Games in Athens. This was the largest number of countries that has ever attended an Olympic Games. At the first modern Olympic Games in Athens in 1896, only 14 countries competed. Australia and Greece are the only countries to have competed at every modern Olympic Games.

Olympic champions – men

These five men have won the most gold medals at the summer Olympic Games.

Athlete	Event	Gold medals
Ray Ewry (USA)	track and field	10
Paavo Nurmi (Finland)	track and field	9
Mark Spitz (USA)	swimming	9
Carl Lewis (USA)	track and field	9
Sawao Kato (Japan)	gymnastics	8

Olympic champions – women

Women first competed in tennis and golf at the Paris Olympic Games in 1900. How things have changed! This table features the five women who have won the most gold medals at the summer Olympic Games.

Athlete	Event	Gold medals
Larissa Latynina (USSR)	gymnastics	9
Jenny Thompson (USA)	swimming	8
Birgit Fischer (Germany)	canoe/kayak	8
Vera Caslavska (Czechoslovakia)	gymnastics	7
Kristin Otto (East Germany)	swimming	6

Top 10 countries – summer Olympic Games

This table lists the top 10 medal-winning countries for the summer Olympic Games. Note that the Soviet Union (now Russia) is the former **Communist** Russian Federation. East Germany is now part of a reunited Germany.

Country	Total medals	Gold medals
USA	4641	892
Soviet Union (USSR)	2118	395
Great Britain	1256	185
Germany	1160	174
France	1156	185
Italy	1006	182
Hungary	898	157
Sweden	885	137
East Germany	846	153
Australia	765	120

Top 10 countries – winter Olympic Games

Listed below are the top 10 medal-winning countries for the winter Olympic Games. Australia first competed at the 1936 winter Olympic Games and has won a total of six medals.

Country	Total medals	Gold medals
Norway	584	99
USA	459	79
Soviet Union (USSR)	407	78
Germany	386	69
Austria	353	51
Finland	293	42
Sweden	249	46
Canada	236	38
Switzerland	225	37
East Germany	223	39

The Olympic rings were designed in 1914 by Baron de Coubertin. The five rings stand for the five regions of the world – Oceania, the Americas, Africa, Europe and Asia. The rings were first used in 1920 at the Olympic Games in Antwerp, Belgium.

Olympic Games timeline

The Olympic Games began more than 3300 years ago. This timeline shows the key events in the long history of the Olympic Games and how they were reborn in modern times.

Before 1300 BCE
The first Olympic Games are held at Olympia.

Before 800 BCE
The original Olympic Games die out.

In 800 BCE
King Iphitos of Elis restarts the Olympic Games at Olympia. Sportsmen from all over Greece compete.

776 BCE
The Greeks start to number the games, which are held every four years. The games of 776 BCE are number one, or the first **Olympiad**.

146 BCE
The Romans **invade** Greece and take over the Olympic Games.

388 AD
The last of the **ancient** Olympic Games is held.

393 AD
Roman **emperor**, Theodosius I, bans the Olympic Games.

Around 400 AD
An earthquake causes the Alpheios River to flood Olympia, which is buried under **tonnes** of mud.

1766
Englishman Richard Chandler visits Olympia and finds some ruins of the ancient games site.

1829
French archaeologists dig at Olympia and discover ruins of an ancient temple, which they ship back to France. Greece bans all digging at the site.

1859
A rich Greek man, Evangelios Zappas, gives money for a major sporting competition in Greece. These games are named the Zappeion Olympics.

1870 and 1875
Second and third Zappeion Olympics are held in Greece.

1875
German **archaeologists** persuade Greece to let them dig at Olympia again.

1876–1889
Ruins of **temples**, sports training grounds and stadiums are discovered at Olympia.

1892
Baron Pierre de Coubertin suggests the Olympic Games should be restarted. His idea is to hold the modern Olympic Games every four years in different cities around the world.

23 June 1894
The **Congress** for the Re-establishment of the Olympic Games, organised by Baron de Coubertin, is held in Paris. The International Olympic Committee (IOC) is set up at this meeting.

1896
The first modern Olympic Games are held in Athens, Greece.

1916
The Olympic Games are not held because of World War I.

1924
The first winter Olympic Games are held in Chamonix, France.

1937
Baron de Coubertin dies. His heart is buried at Olympia.

1940 and 1944
The Olympic Games are not held because of World War II.

1948
Games for People with Spinal Injuries are held in Aylesbury, England, at the same time as the London Olympic Games.

1960
The first Paralympic Games are held in Rome.

1972
Terrorists kidnap and kill 11 Israeli athletes during the Munich Olympic Games in Germany.

1988
The Paralympic Games in Seoul, South Korea, are the first to be held straight after the summer Olympic Games and to use the same venues.

1994
The winter Olympic Games are held in a separate year – halfway between the summer Olympic Games – for the first time.

2008
The Beijing Olympic Games are the first to be held in China.

Find out more

Using the Internet

Explore the Internet to learn more about the Olympic events featured in this book. Websites can change so if the links below no longer work, use a reliable search engine, such as http://yahooligans.yahoo.com or http://www.kids.net.au, and type in the keywords, such as the name of a person, place or event.

Websites

www.olympic.org
The official website of the Olympic Movement contains information on the modern Olympic Games, including history, descriptions of every Olympic sport, a full list of medal winners, Olympic news, and much more.

www.databaseolympics.com
This website has statistics on every modern summer and winter Olympic Games, including medal tally tables and medal winners.

www.perseus.tufts.edu/Olympics/
This site is a little difficult in its wording, but it has excellent information on the ancient Olympic Games. It features a virtual tour of Olympia, champions' stories, descriptions of ancient events and frequently asked questions.

Books

Gaff, J. *Ancient Olympics* Heinemann Library, Oxford, 2004
This book explores the ancient Olympic Games and enables students to link the origins of the Games to their modern equivalent.

Kristy, D. *De Coubertin's Olympics* Lerner Publications Company, Minneapolis, 1995
This interesting, easy-to-read book tells the full story of Baron Pierre de Coubertin and how he re-established the Olympic Games.

Woff, R. *The Ancient Greek Olympics* British Museum Press, London, 1999
Written by a respected historian and teacher at the British Museum, this is a lively, day-by-day description of the ancient Olympic Games. It features excellent pictures and quotes from eyewitnesses.

Glossary

AD stands for *Anno Domini*, meaning 'in the year of the Lord'. Year 1 is the traditional birth of Jesus Christ. The year 2000 AD is 2000 years after the birth of Christ.

altar a flat-topped stone for making offerings to gods

amateur a person who competes for enjoyment, not money

ancient very old; in a time long past

aquatics water sports

archaeologist a person who finds and studies ancient ruins and art

armour a metal body covering used for protection in a fight

BCE stands for 'before the common (or current) era' and replaces the old term, BC ('before Christ'). Year 1 is the traditional birth of Jesus Christ. BCE years are the years before year 1, and are counted backwards. 1300 BCE is 1300 years before the birth of Christ.

bout a sporting contest between two fighters

boycott to avoid or ban

chariot an ancient horse-drawn cart

Christian a person who believes in the teachings of Christ

column a tall cylinder that holds up a roof or arch in a building

combat fighting

communist a person who believes in a political system in which most property is publicly owned and each person works for the benefit of all in the community or state

congress a formal meeting of representatives of nations

discus a heavy, round, flat disc used in sporting event of the same name

drachma the unit of money used in ancient Greece

dressage a kind of horse-and-rider ballet with moves to music

emperor the ruler of an empire

entwine to wind around

equestrian horse-riding events

expert a person with special skill or knowledge

honour to highly respect

hostage held captive or against one's will

invaded seized control of another place or country by force

ivory a material made from the tusks of elephants

javelin a lightweight spear

knocked out knocked unconscious by a blow to the head

Latin the ancient language of Rome

motto a slogan; words expressing an ideal

Nazi a member of the political party, which between 1933 and 1945, under Adolf Hitler, controlled all the cultural, economic and political activities of the German people in an attempt to make Germany the dominant world power

noble good and moral

oath a vow or promise

ode a kind of poem

Olympiad a four-year period between each Olympic Games. Each four-year period is counted as one Olympiad

opponent another competitor in a sporting contest

Palestinians people from Palestine, a country next to Israel

pentathlon (ancient) a five-event sport held at the ancient Olympic Games in which athletes competed in discus and javelin throwing, long jumping, running and wrestling

pentathlon (modern) a five-event sport in which athletes must compete in shooting, riding, swimming, horse riding and running events.

pick a tool used to crush stones

pitch a throw in baseball or softball

prayer a request made to a god

proclaimed announced

racism a bad feeling between different races; belief in the superiority of a particular race over all others

religious festival a celebration for gods

Romans people from ancient Rome

shuttlecock a feathered ball used in badminton

spectator person watching an event

sprint a short, fast race

strigil a metal tool used by sportsmen at Olympia to scrape sand off their bodies

synchronised done at exactly the same time

temple a building for prayer or worship

terrorism organised attacks on civilians and others designed to cause extreme fear

toboggan a long, narrow sled used for going downhill over snow or ice

tonne a unit of mass equal to 1000 kilograms

tragedy a very sad event

vaulting high leaping or jumping

31

Index

Lillehammer
Oslo
Helsinki
Stockholm
Moscow
London
Amsterdam
Berlin
Antwerp
St Moritz
Paris
Munich
Chamonix
Garmisch-Partenkirchen
Albertville
Innsbruck
Grenoble
Sarajevo
Turin
Cortina-d'Ampezzo
Barcelona
Rome
Athens
Olympia

Beijing
Sapporo
Seoul
Nagano
Tokyo

Sydney
Melbourne

MELVILLE SENIOR HIGH SCHOOL
LIBRARY

※ Summer Olympic Games
❄ Winter Olympic Games

N

0   2000   4000 km